INST.

The Easter Story

Rub over the picture for a surprise!

Retold by Laura Kelly

Illustrated by Rick Brown

Jesus and his friends were traveling to Jerusalem for the passover meal. Jesus told two of his friends to go to the village ahead and bring something back for him.

*What did they bring him? Rub to find out.

As Jesus rode into Jerusalem, people began shouting, "Hosanna! Blessed is he who comes in the name of the Lord!" They also spread some things in Jesus' path.

*What did the people put in Jesus' path? Rub to find out.

Jesus went to the temple in Jerusalem. Many people came to hear him teach. Some of them were jealous of Jesus and angered by his teaching. These enemies of Jesus secretly planned to have him arrested and killed.

*Jesus' enemies were called Pharisees.
What did they look like? Rub to find out.

Judas was one of Jesus' followers. He knew that Jesus' enemies wanted to arrest him. Judas said he would help Jesus' enemies if they gave him a bag of something.

*What did Jesus' enemies give Judas? Rub to find out.

Jesus and his friends ate the Passover meal together. Then Jesus did something to help his friends see that they should serve others.

*What did Jesus do? Rub to find out.

After their meal, Jesus and his friends went to the Garden of Gethsemane. Jesus spent the night praying.

*What did his friends do? Rub to find out.

Jesus knew he would be arrested soon. It was God's plan for him to die for the wrongs of everyone who would ever live.

*Who came to arrest Jesus? Rub to find out.

Jesus' friends were afraid when they saw Jesus being arrested.

*What did they do? Rub to find out.

Jesus' enemies didn't believe that he was God. They put him to death on a cross. As Jesus died, something happened to the sky.

*What happened? Rub to find out.

Three days after Jesus died, women visited his tomb. The large stone in front of the tomb had been rolled away and Jesus was gone!

While they wondered about this, someone appeared and said "Do not be afraid. Go and tell my brothers to go to Galilee; there they will see me."

*Who appeared to the women? Rub to find out.

After Jesus' death, his friends were afraid that they would be arrested too. They hid together in a house. Then, someone brought good news that Jesus was alive!

*Who brought the good news? Rub to find out.

But Jesus' friends didn't believe it. "How could Jesus be alive?" they wondered. Peter and John wanted to find out for themselves.

*What did they do? Rub to find out.

When they reached the tomb they saw
something that amazed them.

* What did Peter and John see? Rub to find out.

Sometime later, someone else came to the house where Jesus' friends were hiding. No one could believe their eyes when they saw who it was.

*Who was it? Rub to find out.

Sometime later, it was time for Jesus to leave. As Jesus' friends watched him go up to heaven, someone told them, "Jesus will return some day just the way you saw him leave."

*Who said this? Rub to find out.